I Thought You Would Be Shelter

I Thought You Would Be Shelter

Men Poems

Catherine Ferguson

SUNSTONE PRESS

SANTA FE

Sunstone books may be purchased for educational, business, or sales promotional use.
For information please write: Special Markets Department, Sunstone Press,
P.O. Box 2321, Santa Fe, New Mexico 87504-2321.
Body typeface › Caslon Pro
Printed on acid-free paper

Library of Congress Cataloging-in-Publication Data

Names: Ferguson, Catherine, 1947- author.
Title: I thought you would be shelter : men poems / by Catherine Ferguson.
Description: Santa Fe : Sunstone Press, 2017.
Identifiers: LCCN 2017022788 | ISBN 9781632931740 (softcover : acid-free
   paper)
Classification: LCC PS3606.E722 A6 2017 | DDC 811/.6--dc23
LC record available at https://lccn.loc.gov/2017022788

SUNSTONE PRESS IS COMMITTED TO MINIMIZING OUR ENVIRONMENTAL IMPACT ON THE PLANET. THE PAPER USED IN THIS BOOK IS FROM RESPONSIBLY MANAGED FORESTS. OUR PRINTER HAS RECEIVED CHAIN OF CUSTODY (COC) CERTIFICATION FROM: THE FOREST STEWARDSHIP COUNCIL™ (FSC®), PROGRAMME FOR THE ENDORSEMENT OF FOREST CERTIFICATION™ (PEFC™), AND THE SUSTAINABLE FORESTRY INITIATIVE® (SFI®). THE FSC® COUNCIL IS A NON-PROFIT ORGANIZATION, PROMOTING THE ENVIRONMENTALLY APPROPRIATE, SOCIALLY BENEFICIAL AND ECONOMICALLY VIABLE MANAGEMENT OF THE WORLD'S FORESTS. FSC® CERTIFICATION IS RECOGNIZED INTERNATIONALLY AS A RIGOROUS ENVIRONMENTAL AND SOCIAL STANDARD FOR RESPONSIBLE FOREST MANAGEMENT.

WWW.SUNSTONEPRESS.COM
SUNSTONE PRESS / POST OFFICE BOX 2321 / SANTA FE, NM 87504-2321 /USA
(505) 988-4418 / ORDERS ONLY (800) 243-5644 / FAX (505) 988-1025

Dedication

For the men:

My most special poet friend, James McGrath, with whom I have been writing and sharing the joy of life for many years, who encouraged me to make this book possible;

For Tom Lennox, poet now deceased, who worked with my writings and said to me "I think you should put together a book of *Men Poems*";

For Ron MacDonald, the first man in my life, his deep heart.

For the women:

Artist Judy Tuwalestiwa who helped me edit these poems;

Joan Logghe, who inspired me with the ecstasy of poetry;

Anne Valley-Fox who delights me with her lovely talent and humor;

poets Katherine Seluja and Colleen Carias who have shared many a Wednesday poetry morning with me for years now;

Maria Cristína Lopez, whose intelligence guides me like a star;

Carla, Priscilla and Denise, Lisa, Barbara... women of such strength and talent, you make me so glad to be in this world.

Contents

Preface

I wrote this book because I found myself with notebooks full of poems about the incredibly rich relationships in my life. It is the search most humans have, to be "met," complemented, joined, married. It is everyone's journey, to love, to want to be loved. In expressing myself with pen and paper I experienced catharsis and some reconciliation for the horror of loss.

When my father committed suicide before I was two years old, I endured the original trauma, the "sickly and gangrenous void" as well as the void in my mother's heart. My father became God, who was also up there in heaven holding a paintbrush. But I wanted him down here on earth. I felt like a being cut in half.

At puberty, I discovered boys and felt more complete in their presence. I was attracted to teachers, anyone inspiring who was male and helped me not feel so alone. My mother's stories about boyfriends were romantic, so I learned romance, and added it to my experiences.

It was a spiritual and sensual quest, to feel whole. I wanted to be in relation to the other half of myself, whoever it might be. But I discovered that for all my dreams of wanting to be whole and sheltered, my pattern was mostly to choose the wrong man.

I can only imagine that readers might empathize with my quest, enjoy the rich detail of events as remembered in love, and find that the peace I feel in later years might be seen as hope for renewal, joy in the wonder of life.

The reader may expect ultimately a book of praise, that it is possible to get to know and love the object of one's desire, to travel a path with the Other, to feel part of all nature when one finds a friend, no matter how long it lasts.

Reading each poem takes me back in time to the ecstasy, the bewilderment, the sorrow, to the rich physical life that was and is mine.

This collection of poems was written over the course of twenty years, or more. As time goes by, I am more at peace within myself, no longer craving a male figure to save me or make me feel whole. I am whole. It took all these poems to get there.

Poetry is a way to stop time. For a moment, for the length of a poem, the reader is any age, is all women, all men. Poetry offers the human planet a way to connect deeply to one another's inner worlds. I have been lucky to know many writers who have shared their work and encouraged me to open my heart to them.

Foreword

At last, adventures beyond the world that become handrails on the foggy bridge where we hold bits of our life, where we can sigh, Yes! together with the poet.

Catherine Ferguson combines memory and imagination to recreate the real world of relationships where we can join her to walk safely while breaking every eggshell we ever painted. Catherine writes in that creative space between the people she loves and her inner arena, a space where we might dwell when fully alive.

In "Motel Six" she muses:

I slide into the other bed,
pull the sterile sheet
up to my ears.
You will see me only
by TV light.

She asks in her poem "Do You Want To Be Married By Fire Or Ice"?

In "Journals" she declares:

I am seventeen.
I have a head like a mountain lion. So there.
I can tell you she wears a Mexican blouse
and pleated skirt while I lie with him
on the green grass.

In "No One Can Say, I'm Sorry, He's Busy" she finds:

I find you beside me in the evenings
looking over my shoulder as I draw.
Your thumb print blurs the sharp edges

> *I wrap around everything.*
> *Now you talk to me the way*
> > *fire talks, the way dryness aches*
> *in the branches.*

In "Tree House" she wants:

> *I want to wake up in a kiss*
> *in the sweet emptiness*
> *that lives after the grave.*

In "The House Of The Woman Wants You To Know" she knows:

> *I have learned to say*
> *<u>no father. No father</u> to the owl in the tree,*
> *<u>no father</u> to the gypsies in the park,*
> *<u>no father</u> to the gangrenous void.*

This is a collection to fold down the corners of the pages as you are reading to remember, admitting, *<u>I live here.</u>*

This is a gathering of ghosts to hold as you look into your mirror, admitting, *<u>I know you.</u>*

Catherine helps us to define ourselves, to include those parts of ourselves given to us by fully loving another human being.

Catherine Ferguson has created a book that clears away the darkness of any shadow that might block the light from discovering the names on the map we have drawn to move about the earth loving who we meet on the journey.

—James McGrath
Santa Fe, New Mexico

I
Above Us the Willows Bend

Pause

You are holding me in your arms.
Above us the willows bend in a warm wind.
You have wiped the grease off your hands.
You have crawled out from under a nightmare
for one piercing moment of love.

I look straight at the camera without a flicker
because the eye is my mother in her gathered skirt.
You carry me in a basket and gently lay me down.
She is worried you won't know what to do with me,
but you know.

I watch you light the kerosene lamp, pick up
Lorca's poem about the highwaymen.
Your agony stretches through the rooms of the tiny
house, but this afternoon the sad nocturne
abandons you.

You are festive as your eyes smile at me.
I see a halo around your head. Light bursts
like cellophane and it is ten years later.

I sit on the porch in Scottsdale coloring inside
black outlines on newsprint. I have learned to say
no father. No father to the owl in the tree, *no father*
to the gypsies in the park, *no father* to the sickly
and gangrenous void.

My mother pushes through the screen door
wearing olive-green pedal pushers. She has found
a tiger's eye in the grass under the eucalyptus tree.
I look at its light. I've seen that eye before.
When *you-no-father* held me in that pause.

College Rain

Even at breakfast my mother waited for someone,
perhaps my father returned from the grave.

I promised my boyfriend that, wherever we were,
if it rained, we would meet by the fountain
in the middle of campus.

I wanted him wet, myself wet, the date palm
and the eucalyptus trees wet.

My mother napped on the floor in the cool hallway.

I waited seismic in front of the dorm,
followed the procession of water ditches
to his silhouette by the fountain.

Nothing fake or false, the first man
who wasn't a dream.

Do You Want to be Married by Fire or Ice?

17

We stand in the kitchen.
He simmers celery and onions.
I mar the ritual; I can't cut the tomatoes right,
I peel away too much of the garlic,
don't shut the cabinet doors
all the way.

He wants the portrait of a marriage.
I make so many mistakes.

He won't be able to combine me
with his family porcelain plates.
I'm out of the kitchen
before dinner is ready.

There are no guarantees.

Before the Fact

I wanted this man
whose waist reminded me of the equator.
I wanted to be wrapped around his waist
like his own belt
and spun.

Flying on airplanes I thought of him,
looked down at quilted woven country,
stylized irrigation and swimming pools,
each rectangle containing him.
Looked for leaks,

tears where I could enter.
One day our bodies walked through each other,
came out the other side.

I was trying to bring all the airplane trips,
the times I felt him in the checkerboard of fields,
in the curved snakes of rivers and highways;
I tried to make a lifetime of turning night into day
giving our moment its true wedding.

Sunlight drew halos all over the cholla.
I felt the thorns as we lay down.

Journals

Friday 2005

My mother wears a purple dress
she bought at the flea market.
Strands of coral and turquoise
twist around her neck.

Sunday 1964

I am seventeen.
I have a head like a mountain lion. So there.
I can tell you she wears a Mexican blouse
        and a pleated skirt while I lie with him
        on the green grass.

Monday 1964

In my white nightgown I fly through the rooms
like an albino bat, my tongue a waterfall.
My mother, in pale blue pajamas, watches TV.

I am getting warmed up, tasting his mouth, tasting it again
to get the real sense, his head on the ground, my fingers in his
dark hair, a current rising in me from the grass, his hand.

Saturday 2005

Momma in brown shorts and striped tee shirt.
We sip the bourbon she keeps below the sink.
It tastes like his mouth. His back spreads on the inside

of my mind. His hand fills me. Grass tickles.
I have a throat like a snake, memory like a hurricane.
I pour the man like brown liquor over ice cubes.
The moment when ice catches fire,

steam pours up. She knows when I add water
I add it to the fire within me she can't put out.

I Married a Man Named Van

In my dream there were three Vans;
      one of them a waste of spring,
         one of them a woman inside a man,
            and one of them an old trailer rotting by the river.
In my dream the god said *draw your dream.*
      I drew the man who married me as Diego Rivera.
       I drew the Van who loves woman as a snake.
         I drew the Van who trails behind me as a friend.

In my dream the god said *you can let go completely—*
      then all the Vans will dance around you.
I said: but it was such a waste of dream, of the dance of marriage.
      All those women trailing behind him, and how I couldn't bear
        to draw their faces,
all those countries where I thought I could be one
      with one Van.

In my dream the god said *you cannot lose what you never had.*

Trucks are parked on the lonely beach.
Women are cooking in the trailer behind the horsetail swamp.
I am picking up one fair seashell
after another.

Spring

I think about morning in that house.
You must have noticed how I dragged
the furniture around while you were
at work so I could make the bed
the night before,

                      so you could wake
to pink walls and me, standing on my head,
white blossoms on the wild cherry
out the window.

                 Quick, I'll love you
before your feet hit the layers of old linoleum,
before you reach for the crossword puzzle.

A slight wind lifts the dried grasses
from the bureau where I placed them
in loose arrangements for you to admire,
to identify with your magnifying glass,
your fingers holding each stem to the light.

Quick, I'll love you before you make the coffee,
before you open the door to exclamations
hanging like stars in the cherry tree.

Her Neighbor, the *Santero*

She has become the *santera*, keeper of secrets.
    Perhaps the juncos love her, as they mark her white gessoed boards
        the way they mark the snow over his footprints.

She adds cosmos and petunias to the borders of the icons
    which seem to paint themselves, San Jose and Santa Lucia.
        She hears prayer inside each breast, splatters her blood

on top of the mesa in the background. She hears him stamp on the ant hills
    with his sharp-toed boots. The brim of his hat, a few pine needles,
        sun rising behind the driveway beginning the day,

what she counts on. Not coffee or the round kitchen table. Someone
    has to love the little frown from the other side of her sleep,
        while death roams the property.

She becomes unrecognizable to herself. Someone has to paint all those retablos,
    face after face. Wash out the brushes. But she can't remember
        her mother's face!

He's so good at depicting the holy sainted gesture, Saint Francis in the shade.
    He dies seven days a week into a horse, a wagon, waffles, a bathtub.
        He stops peering in her window.

He doesn't hear the *flap* of newly-washed hair onto her breasts from the shower.
    They have been fighting but now they are painting.
        He wants to be two *santeros* on one horse first thing in the morning.

The small patio will not give him back.

Come Round to My House
(He Thinks of Her)

She keeps a basket for emergency—
　　　lavender, garlic cloves, rib bones
　　　from small rodents, needles from lacebark pine,
　　　old embroidery needles—

I wake with her scent sewed into me,
　　　eat bread with honey, walk through mint
　　　　　shirtless to the truck.

I pretend I don't see her standing in the dirt,
　　　barefoot, watching me from the back. Pretend
　　　　　I don't see her hair, the sad eyes of her garden,
　　　　　　　borders and careful
　　　stemming of paths, full-blown pale lilac.

Her eyes not the color of mud or chocolate—
　　　the available nut browns—
　　　but ink black
　　　with the closed-in fire

　　　of a dreamy nursery rhyme, hard to fathom.
　　　in a roomful of breathing
　　　under the fan and pots of geraniums.

Deeper than Money

I know you.
You wake from your nap at 3:30 or 4:00,
look out at the lack of rain, shake your head.

You check the small refrigerator,
pull out the ice from the over-frosted freezer,

spread out the newspaper,
scan the car ads, study the sales at Home Depot,
your mouth pursed in evaluation.

You are oblivious
to the feral four o'clock plants.

If you were to glance at the sky, apricot opening,
the glory of it would surprise you—

the thought of you catches in my throat.

But I Had Agreed

Up against the unplastered wall with vows to be said,
what could they say at my wedding—
fifty years old, still that bad child who likes to kiss.

A hundred velvet shadows beckoned from outside of me,
the inside reflected water left in the wheelbarrow.
I was tangled like the hose snaking around the side of the house.

Married would be the white paint peeling off the utility room wall,
the bell that would ring once the vow was murmured.
I waited at the blue door of his house to be faithful

to his lisp, to his unmatched socks.
Married would be a song like thread winding up
all the years with grass inside. I was ready to use
his name, his hairbrush, his secrets and his towel.

A hundred velvet shadows on the inside,
his weight crushing the story I would tell.

Snowman

View through the cracked windshield,
my face, as usual, in the side mirror.

He is no longer my boyfriend but the habit of love remains:
his two children, the way we spent weekends.

Truck motor runs as I jump in the cab.
Snow drifts across the dirt road,
clumps in gnarled leafless trees, on boulders.

The man makes a fire. Air trills with singing juncos,
the white of their tail feathers like parentheses in the frosted banks.

I watch us paint the picture of how we used to be.

I still know how to hold the little girl to my chest,
kiss her soft cold cheek, wet with wisps of hair.

The boy peels a globe of snow from the ground.
Towards the fire and away again.
Three big balls become a man we have never met before,

light bouncing off his woolen cap. We twist a cigarette package
into his grin.

Ice cracks in the river.

I hold the boy's small coarse hands in mine, smell his wet scent,
look into his eyes, big with questions.

Snow covers our tracks around the fire,
covers up the land and the way we had changed our lives.
I look at the flakes shining on the man's dark bare head.

Put out the fire.

Our breath fogs the inside of the truck windows,
our laughter streams as he drives me home.

II
Touch the Bark

Heavy Equipment

I stopped going to my grandma's house
on Sundays.
I didn't miss the Gambel's quail in the vinca
or the agave's pointed thorns
in the driveway.

I just wanted to rub cheekbones and gnaw
on his chin.
I wanted to learn new things and stay in that mood
where you excavate a big chair in a dark room.

My grandma still went to church and wore the black mantilla.
I wasn't beside her to be hugged and introduced
after the money went around.
I wasn't there to watch the clouds rise
like dinosaurs above Camelback Mountain.

I didn't want to paint pink flowers with tendrils
on the black rocking chair.

I just wanted to play *drive me* and *tow me.*
I wanted,
   I just wanted
someone besides my grandma to wrench me down
under the grapefruit tree.

The first kiss he got was like one I'd give my grandma.
The next kiss was like a back hoe tearing up the earth.

Of course I ended up crying a lot
against the custard-colored fence.

Of course I wish I could have stayed a granddaughter
playing on the woven mat, pushing mesquite pods
into the mud wall of desert.

Photographs Never Taken

Here is the bed, newly made. Here is the moon, half-full,
  my mother naked on the *serape* as he stands behind the waiting
canvas, her body vague as mist in the underpaint.
  She's hurt because he has disappeared inside his gaze.
Only when a spark of his match strikes the raised hills of her spine
  does she sigh.

A sudden light in the middle of a field,
  linden tree filled with crows, tequila in a shot glass,
glistening vocabulary of paint.
  I am born nine months later.

  His wife holds the baby. He reaches for gin, listens to a horse
neighing on the horizon. He swallows, feels the pulse
  that will make another baby, the rush of traffic
   that will never stop.

Motel 8

I do not want you naked and huge
on the motel queen-sized bed--
hair spread out on the sheet,
small motel glass
full to the top with whiskey.

I get in the other queen bed,
put the sterile sheet
up to my ears.
You will see me only
by TV light.

You sigh and read your car chase mystery
long after I've turned off Popeye.

I can't sleep with the glare from your individual nite lite.

In the morning you lie on your side,
head facing the wall,
profile outlined on the pillowcase.
Still I do not want you,
the sheet below your shoulders
more modest now, still I don't need
to unwrap your sleeping feet
as if I were living in the moment
and still had those ideas.

Christmas 1962

Inside:
>first boyfriend, bliss blossom.
>>My mother doesn't like him. I do.
>>>Kisses like white wafers.

Outside:
>we pick up Aunt Judy at the airport.
>>I scan faces, looking for him,
>>>look for the feel of secret skin, for
>>>>Aunt Judy to understand my wonder.

Christmas as exciting
>as my mouth learning. Hush, take up this little baby
>>hush, stop all your silly chatter,
>>>hush, Jesus is being born.

Past midnight I creep out into the yard
>to him. Holy holy night. Baby being born
>>in me. Lie in the stars' bleeding light, my arms
>>>hold this first body as close

as god. Nothing between me and desire. In my belly
>carols sing, my legs offering.

Rachmaninoff 1965

In the back room of the house, you led me up stairs
to arrive at Rachmaninoff, dancing my insides
on a platform which lifted
         and then, when I felt myself higher,
            lifted me louder
               and then
                       higher and louder.

Walls glistening with grass, creosote scent,
Inca doves fluttering over the bed, soft wings gliding
along your eyelids, and mine, humming desert stars.

Downstairs someone slammed the screen door.
Sunset filled the window. I walked up more steps,
daring my arms to hold back.

Where was my dress? The one I kept on long enough for you
to take off? Company waited, smoke curling between their words.
I lifted, shimmered on top of the radio overlooking
the far blue mountains, hovered on the edge of a forest fire,
flames rising up the backs of my thighs.

You clasped your belt, smoothed your blond hair
off your high cheekbones.
We'd loved so much I thought you were me.

In the living room, I fidgeted on the red couch
while you smoked a joint.

I wanted you back in bed
teaching me about the flutes of my arms,
the ocotillo wands of my backbone,
sudden waterfalls pouring out of rock ledges—
deer in sunlight, the harder I closed my eyes.

An Allegiance Only to Currents

Please hurry
so I have something to cling to,
so there will be meaning
to all that my body records
as I peak in one supreme
fusion of two dreams.

I open your hands,
place them on my face.
I see the crease in your forehead,
I see the rain in your eyes.

Afterwards,
I want to be alone
until I need you again.
You must understand,
my desire to write it all down.
While you lie sated with love.

San Miguel

San Miguel's Scales:
    The Weighing Machine
        Of the Soul

San Miguel speaks:
    I weigh *you*
    and your moon phases--
    wife, girlfriend, morning pain--

    against your husband's weight,
    his absence,
    his shoes not there,
    his alarm clock silenced.

    I insist you tell me
    your nightmares,
    how the wheat felt against your back
    when he lay down with you
    in the field.

Ghost Visitor

January. Northern New Mexico. Cold nips my
shoulders through sweater and jacket, every few days
another version of frozen stems, shocked flower heads.

Logs huddle in stacks by the front door, shadows
of limbs quiver along the ground, wind
shifts the leaves in eddies along the coyote fence, lifts

the juniper boughs off the stone wall. When I step outside,
I think I hear his truck humming in the driveway,
exhaust rising in clouds of smoke winters long ago.

I begin to move towards him. My voice floats
over the stones in the border between wizened purple
crabapples and clustered hawthorn berries

reflected in his sunglasses. A finch, its belly bright
with carmine blood, flits and pulses noisily in the dense

cedar. I hear the twang of country music from his truck
radio, and the passenger door swinging open as the engine
idles and his toothless grin begins the dry rasping

of a dead man's patter—only the soughing
of heavy cottonwood branches. His ghost twists
the cigarette filter, throws it through the open window,

reminds me of a 4th of July, crack of thunder
interrupting an afternoon party on Canyon Road,
horse rearing in the rain outside the fence.

I imagine him now clinging to that great animal, wearing
his yellow slicker, water pouring over his face
and into his eyes like tears.

Snow falls. Pine Siskins flock in little clouds
of breezy streaked twitters. A wind pushes the juniper
so hard I see through it to the road.

I retreat back in the house, out of the mist and smoke.

It Can Be Eaten

Once I offered my hand; it can be eaten I said,
fingers dipped in chocolate, which one of me have you chosen?
The fury, hair tangled like drowned spider webs, or the wild-fowl?
I refuse your pity, I would rather leave
than lock away the dark red sun we opened.

Once I offered my mouth, to be swallowed by the fish.
I was lost in the dark cave of your belly.
Your scales can be eaten I said, tasting the inner edge
of your wrist, then the center.

You vomited me whole from the lonely place.
I fell shattered, trembling, cradling my red sun.
It warmed me.

I was full and self-contained, held in place
by my furious power,
red sun between my legs
and my memory.

*   *   *

Once I offered my life, *it can be eaten,* I said,
*dip me once in the chocolate river and once again
in the cold pond.*
Which one will I choose?
The furious wild-fowl or the fish?

You refuse my pity, you would rather leave
than destroy the red sun we exposed.

Once you offered your mouth to teach me to kiss.

Your life can be eaten, I say, tasting the inner edge.

Bicentennial Year

The year of the white truck I painted like an American flag
when we didn't own a vehicle, but walked hip to hip down Canyon
Road,

slept in the sunken room, colors of Greece, blue and white,
one night on the roof saw figures dancing, tall as Shalako,
till dawn bloodied the sky.

I never dared imagine what wine, what black telephone,
what oil painting of him lying naked reading *Esquire* would disappear
over the slope of the way decisions are made, like cutting hair,
a snip here, snip there—even my laugh changed,
and his hair, and our address: at first the same on another street,
then separate.

The year of the snow that fell all too often
when I was angry and he threw the cement table through the TV.

Until I understood that you can only take so much from a man
and then he will ride out of town on his motorcycle.

Swallows fill the room where we slept.

She sleeps with him now
in a room with three cacti in an orange bowl
which I walk around and around.

May

Dusk drizzling lilac and wind
through an open window.
He sang.
I was beside him.

While we talked he stroked the guitar.
Neither of us got up to leave.
Toward morning, electric graze of arms meeting, darting away.

His wrist on my wrist, held on, lay back.
Lazily brushed my cheeks with his lips,
my ears.

Miles between me and sleep.

I am so south of him now,
and the light.

Apples and Dresses

The dress at 4 pm
I am having a seizure of heat

Green dress, as green as apples
I let you eat it off me

We learn each other's histories
Your's, Panama
heat—

I've been there

Dresses not apples
not the color of apples
hang in the closet

Spell *girl*

It's too hot
but I dream about
apples

III
Peel the Bark Away

No One Can Say, I'm Sorry, He's Busy

I returned, but they had already taken you.

     All day and all night I called.
     They did not let me speak to you.

     Your words strangled by that rattle.
     Your hands, searching tentacles,
       pulling at the sheets.
     I have seen dying before.
     The eyes innocent and surprised.
     Nothing to say.

I find you beside me in the evenings,
looking over my shoulder as I draw.
Your thumb print blurs the sharp edges
I wrap around everything.
Now you talk to me the way
fire talks, the way dryness aches
in tree branches.

Reference

It is Tucson
     she is hot and no longer wears
anything under her dress
     metaphysics hovers in the fan
she wants to paint
     in spite of two glasses and a bottle
of wine   she is in relation to
     him   to loneliness   her childhood
with its Mexican accent   she is growing
     an alphabet inside her skin
language of his voice
     she wants to paint before the crash
and stampede of his presence
     wants to hold to the fortune of
her privacy but the pigeons on
     the roof   the professor's mustache
the gorgeous skin beside his ears
     remind her of music and all
her arguments for solitary life
     are extinct in the face of his
unembellished nudity which she
     studies as she performs each act
of creation on the canvas
     and simultaneously on the telepathic
flesh of his being   always
     in relation she is waking to her roots
which carry her down into
     her father's colors   his
meditation below the earth into
     his madness she is sure the earth
loves her even though she is
     always in relation to the hour   his
voice   the dogs and the fan

Yes

You were the dark window. I thought I was still lit like a bedroom.
I could not separate you from the fallen star.

I reached for you as if you were a photograph streaming with light.
I moved my furniture out of the way of your body.

You spent a long time in the shower.
My body sheltered a beast.

  What was the temperature of my privacy?

So many Fridays inventing what lips do with hands.
What I did with the trumpets of your fingers, the black flute of your throat.
You, the entire summer of opera.

  I once lived for taste after taste, crescendo in your mouth.
  Your kiss, how far I shine.

Coins fell on the floor as I sat on your lap.

  Are the mean parts of you because your mother was sad?

Your answer is a bat fluttering the dark. Your answer is your mother's silence,
  her chipped antique bowls, sepia print of your Dutch grandmother.

  Not taught in the classroom. The tongue's honey, flavor of mother,
  begins to taste like waking after a terrible dream. That biggest sleep.

Your mother's handprints stain my lungs.

Santa Fe, First Days

> I stood on his threshold, heard
a lonely tune from my childhood.

I sang with it long and low.

Then I unpacked and began to paint my life.
I knew where to lay my clothes.

Before I met him I already knew how his dark eyes
reflected one point of light from the windowsill.
I knew his shaving brush, a relic in its nicho above the
sink.
I knew the moon peering through the skylight
over his bed, bleaching his hand where it lay on my hip.

I recognized the heavy red blanket,
the weight pulling my body towards his.
I recognized the bitterness.

I ran barefoot in the snow
from his house to mine.
Night closed around me.
The lamp burned too bright.

Father's Day

I brought flowers,

showed him white asters
in the center, smelling like the overripe papaya
on his hands before he married.

His eyes on the first orange lily,
blue spikes of penstemon,
loose pink Bonica rose
opened with scent of honey.

Yellow evening primrose,
chunky stem with globes of unopen blossoms,
pointed to leaves in ladders.

I wanted him to paint the flowers
on canvas from the market,

to fill the gray bucket of his Pennsylvania childhood.
When he stood by the tall statue of a nude woman
in Mexico city

I drew his eyes,
tearing the paper as I outlined dark brown like mine,
but large like my sister's.

One Bite at a Time

on your ear, in the hollow of your neck
blue shadows of flowers.
Buds pressed in your skin by me,
which you admitted you hated.

Take time out for tequila and ribs at Maria's,
the waiter with long hair pulled back;
I could lean into the ashy counter and wound him
as I wounded you, a bruise or two
on his shoulder blade, circle of purple sores
surrounding his nipples.

No, I turn away from the waiter.

Our daughters sat across from me in the booth.

Have another margarita.

Chile and beef and blue corn stuffed in my mouth
by the fork held in my hand which has been cradling
you. Yes, I like a man's body when I'm in love.
But I want to brand it.

Have another margarita.

Daughters with their mothers' eyes and their flower mouths
and all their beginnings happening at the table. This man
with his head of crystal, with his hands of ivory, tearing
the sopapilla. Steam flows out of the hollow bread,
I slump into over-drive while he pours honey
into the opening and sucks.

Later I want to be out of the truck.
Between snow to my mid-calf and night as cold and bright
as tinsel, I crave sleep.
Carve the food out of me.
I want to be amputated of you.
I step into aluminum, it is so cool,
so slippery, I want to kiss it.
I want to lie with the little animals that are dead
beneath the powdered sugar.
Leave me alone.
Full-length in the deaf-and-dumb whiteness
finally free.

"Don't Sing Love Songs,
    you'll wake my mother..."
        —Joan Baez, 1962

She lies on her bed
praying for dawn.
Her daughter is breaking
her heart.

Thin bones arch,
empty of the man.
If the mother sleeps, she dreams
he returns from the grave:

walks toward her house in moonlight.
Shrimp plants quiver.
He sees his daughter beneath the grapefruit tree
kissing a boy.

He hesitates, feet balanced
against the break where the cement
becomes grass.
No words, only the hollow sound
of a dead man's love.

The Dogs Are Out

Once you investigated the trap by the river,
drove the truck in reverse straight up the mountain,
found the rock embedded in wood,
laid it near my feet. I picked it up,
held it to the light, then to my heart.

I remember your bracelet
on the chopping block table,
thin as the delicate veins of your wrist.

Water Heater

My father even saw me
with my clothes off.

If I went in the closet
closed the door and sat
by the water heater close
to the floor in the dark,
he was with me.

He never got mad at me.

Blacksmith

That year
when philosophy wore a dress and drank bourbon
in a little silver cup
when I stood between the bookcases of doubt and desire
said I wanted a certain pencil that wrote like a river
and told the truth

when I was afraid of the window that looked out on traffic
but he wasn't afraid and walked naked from door to door
holding the firearm between morning and noon

when I dreamed of conception
drew his profile on the face of a baby girl
saw her following me through the days
carrying my paintbrushes

when I learned about the third dimension
when he helped me carve a hand and the form took shape
out of the soft pine as my own hand blistered and bled

that year
I woke screaming when his foot hit the sheet rhythmically
that year
I called the dark age when soot wore its disguise of a man
who reminded me of my father but would not die

instead would hold me out from himself
like something dripping

Girl Scout Father Daughter Dinner

I felt sorry for anybody
who felt sorry for me.
I felt thin, special.

A father was found for me,
the janitor.
I felt sorry for him.

He wore a suit he was saving
for his funeral.
We ate pigs in the blanket
and Mississippi Mud.

His hands shook when he gave me
the red carnation in his buttonhole.

You Hand Me the Bill

You charge me for the ancient coins
in your suitcase; you dream of sharpened knives
that cut the serving girl's waist.

How many highways will we travel
without getting out of Minneapolis,
or Tampa, Florida?

The little dog tries to comfort me.

Then the crisis of money,
pennies rattling around
on the floor of the car...

How can I possibly love you?

IV
Where Winter Meets Spring

Frying Pan

Stood by the refrigerator imagining
sex. He enters the room, it is morning,
he's so handsome.

What about breakfast?

He wants a hole in the bread, fried with an egg inside.
Maybe I was mad about something. Frying pan steamy.

He takes me in his arms, we lie down.
I see the doorstep's dirty dust,
I stand, use a sponge to wipe it clean, catch his look.
By evening he's acting weird, everything ironic.

But he is so handsome.

We eat at a café. He won't quit flipping things, flips
the straw, the sugar packet, flips the fork, flips
the way we are kind to each other.

Later, I fry two pork chops.

He's outside in the yard connecting the water pipes.
I paint the kitchen wall crimson.

He wakes me after exactly eight hours of sleep.
I make the bed, unmake it, lie still while he dances
in the other room, dances and dances
alone.

Set in My Ways

In Mexico,
when I was sixteen
and angry at my mother,

I stood, surrounded by beggar dogs,
searching for the sugar skull
of my father.

I was impatient at being
anyone's daughter,
cross with my apricot dress
for being too tight,
with the plum colored sandals
for blistering my feet.

I caught a man's eye,
stood in the sun too long,
looked at pictures of saints,
let her worry.

In Mexico, my father conceived me,
left me
to my mother,

left me this habit
of leaving.

Taxco

My father everywhere invisible.
Mountains blue and far away,
I follow my father over the red-tiled roofs,

into the valleys. We dip and sway
with the Sleeping Lady, hear roosters crowing.
My father's voice is the thunder rumbling.
Sky rains on the cobblestones

where we walk, rains on other children,
rains on burros. I take his hand and climb the flower-strewn path
to our house. We hear the pigs squealing.
We stand together at the low wall looking out over Taxco.

Below we spy my mother strolling the streets
with her two daughters, colored ribbons
woven through their braids.

My father points out me to me, walking along
with my mother and sister. We amble in and out
of open-doored shops. We buy *pan dulce.*

I watch later at dinner when a man tears the soft white
caves of the bread, stuffs them into his mouth,
ignores the crust.

Friend of the Family

When I look at the horizon of yellow leaves,
I see him burning.
I smell him in what is cooking,
taste his omelet as my fork enters the flesh
of egg.

           I hear him snore—
siesta—his wife's knees up against his thighs,
and I, faithful friend, wait in another room,
a sentry. I feel him in the rug beneath my feet,
in my body as it arches for a moment.
He does not leave me.

Inhabited by another, I wait in Mexico.
He's painting on the other side of the rock wall
wearing a straw hat decorated with a tassel.
Later he will want tequila.
The music will begin. I will sit in the shadowed hallway
quietly writing in my journal.
Our suitcases will be packed,

his wife's skirts folded flat. I will stare at animals
carved in the wood of the red chest from Michoacan.
I will look at those clay devils he collects,
I will feel his hand call me home from another decade.
Angels and devils perch in the tree of light on the horizon.
Inside me a dead man will not die.
His hunger heats a hunger in me.

How do I hear the music now?
How do I wait in dark rooms with serapes on the wall,
his painting of me still hiding its face with my hand?
How do I stand while he slow dances in me,
while he paints, when his fingers grasp
at all the pretty little things?

Geography

I built a canoe and sailed down the Rio Grande into Mexico.
I looked for my father who wore two or three lives.
I heard that he lived in a cave near Lake Chapala.

I met a professor on his way to Romania,
and a young man who made an arm bracelet for me
out of leather and brass.
I've seen who it is when it's not my father.

I've known how to make life from mud and scratch.

I've known thunder to flood the dry arroyos.

I built a house beneath the cottonwoods on the Galisteo River.
I stopped looking for my father many lives ago.

I've heard that it is possible to follow the Rio Grande into Mexico.

I've seen the beauty of the ten thousandth thirty first dawn.
I've known that I would be alone most of the time.

I slip off into the desert to dance with my father.

Ouija Board

We questioned
the Ouija board in the book-lined room

open to the sea, with Delsey, who was bad,
and Delsey's baby sister who ate marshmallows.
My sister and I took turns. If we let ourselves go
and looked into Delsey's eyes, our hands

moved with the planchette over the board.
We learned we were going to be president,
would be married by age thirteen, have nine
children, become Catholic, eat seaweed, dance

with an octopus. I found out
my father would come back, walk with me
down to the beach, past the Laundromat
and dry cleaners, past *31 Flavors*

and the furniture store with the statues of small
black jockeys in red riding jackets holding big rings,
down the broken sidewalk to the pink cement steps,
salty and dog-peed. My father straight from

the Ouija board would hold my hand and walk with me
up the carpet of light which the setting sun spreads
on the sea.

It Is Not All Right

I stood in the kitchen,
listening.

People sat beside the stove, talking
talking clack talk against the walls—
cancer…incurable…operation…6 weeks…6 days.
Rage slammed
at the cupboards.
People held their mugs,
already deep in This Is,
ready to let him go.

When I visit, his mouth so tight,
not kind or welcoming:
Do you ever think of me?
Do you love me now?

His eyes huge and haunted
by the rain I'll feel on my cheeks.

His hand feels for the tube
which drains a hole in his abdomen.
His look is the last drop falling from a bottle of scotch,
so I kneel on the floor at his feet to empty the bag.

Between us
only the sound of folded plastic,
and somewhere a door closing.

She Leaves His Body

Looking over the crossword at his mouth, concentrating
on words that flew up like small black birds

she knew that time would close like a purse snapping
and that in a sharp wind span she would be alone

mouthing the words that go across, like geese in formation,
words that go down and keep her shut in a crowded corral

of relentless truth. How his tiny writing, bird scratch,
fill-in-the-blanks, would not begin to heal the empty squares,

the clues that would find no meaning, no way to make *kiss* mean
forever or *stay.*

She learns: what the rain writes on the ground
is for her alone.

Sculpting Life

I was making a left at the chamisa,
        a right at the dog.
You were angled thin, broad-shouldered
        against the Russian Olive.

Somebody was saying that I am poor.
Somebody was saying that I am rich.

I said, that doesn't matter. I've never had children.

I spent all day drawing an Oriental poppy.

You looked down at your worn-out boots,
a shadow dissolving your face.
Suddenly squeezing my pencil too tight,
I coughed up my words.
Our baby girl who never—

My love didn't fit in your golden Falcon.
My love didn't fit in your rock and roll.

You lit a cigarette.
Leaving, I turned right at the Santa Fe phlox,
        left at the Indian paintbrush.

Once I Loved You

before I was hungry. It came naturally, the fish
in your basin swimming peacefully were fish
I recognized.

You had forgotten your shoes. You were so light.
Swimming came easily then, and confusing your
body with mine

before I was empty. It came as a surprise, you
riding a horse I did not recognize. You offered
to carry me through the city.

But I was so heavy. Refusing you came naturally
then, and knowing your body from mine

before I was natural. Sewn into my dress by the way
light gathered around a mirror. Easily comfortable
in any chair, on the floor.

I could make love without a bed, as long as my skin
beheld an open window. As long as the dress let in
the light

before I was warm. It came to me naturally, wrapped
sea shell, sea horse, birds flying up out of the sea.
You had forgotten my name.

I had forgotten to swim. The fish walks on land,
searches for your body.

A Dream of Living with a Man in a Different Kind Of Time

Across the desert to the abandoned house we walk.
We do not bring water.
The sun spills on us like hot oil, but I don't mind.

That day still scratches a dream
in my throat.

I see us sitting on that porch.
We aren't afraid of the heat.
Sometimes we wear clothes,
or we are naked.

Sometimes we lie with the lizards stretched along the rocks.
Turning our hips slowly this way and that,
we face sunrise, then sunset.

I see you carrying the water we did not have.
You slowly pour it along the base of my neck, watch it run
down my spine to pool beneath my legs.

The sun might drink the water.
I might move to a room inside the house.
I might gaze out the window.

How many days could we spend in silence?

One word might puncture the afternoon,
a wound gaping in the center of our lives.
We watch the word balance in the air
between us, then burst like a bomb.

Nothing can save us. Nothing on the window sill,
on the mantle, nothing on the long table.

You walk through the door carrying a small stone.
Its blackness rearranges the room.
I search for its home
in your eye.

Tree House

Forgive me.
I made a mistake
in marrying you.

It's all so simple.
Why blend it with the New York Times
or bird journals
when the truth is here and now:
I want to be happy.

I want to wake up in a kiss,
in the sweet emptiness
that lives after the grave.

I want to live in a tree.
I want to eat.
Let me leave with the dog.

Forgive me
for loving you.
The storm pulls west
out of the desert.
My childhood calls me,
Come home.

The House of the Woman Wants You to Know

1
He says:
>I've always loved that house, the deep windows,
>the old blue paint.
>The woman died three weeks ago, I hear her
>calling me from the bedroom.
>It's not right, seeing where she lay, her slippers
>and the little tray on the night table.
>
>I see her husband's hand carving the bedposts,
>her painting on the bed board he made,
>his way with the window frame,
>her way with the color of the walls,
>his carved ceiling beams.

2
I say
as I crawl to your prostrate body,
unwrapping your legs from the stiff vines:
>I want to find a way to make a kiss into a house,
>to make a shared nap last an eternity.

You carve the cross from the pale-skinned pine.
I paint to the edges, where the border starts.
There can be no separating us, here in this house,
now where your slippers lie beside the bed,
where I take off my earrings and place them
in the little tray.

As Red Water Over My Arms

I loved so simply then
the red of blossoms moving into skin
streets running like rivers
in the summer when we laughed
in the gutters
until our dresses were wet
while color dried on the bristles
of my paint brush
and the man who had a problem with time
ducked his tall body low through my small doorway
looking for me

but I was uncovering my eyes
uncovering my ears in the road smelling
of wine and wet rags and sun beating
on perfume
I made everything into a poem
he had to fetch me
carry me inside
he laid me on the floor
his love flowed over my ankles
elbows and knees
slow moving down
a quietness of mermaid
stunned backyard trees hanging
with rain
time was red
then and slow and staining

About the typeface Caslon

Caslon is the name given to serif typefaces designed by
William Caslon I (c. 1692–1766) in London,
or inspired by his work.

Caslon worked as an engraver of punches, the masters used to
stamp the moulds or matrices used to cast metal type.
He worked in the tradition of what is now called old-style
serif letter design, that produced letters with a relatively
organic structure resembling handwriting with a pen.
His typefaces established a strong reputation for their
quality and their attractive appearance.